CONTENTS

ISBN 0-7935-0611-5

7777 West Bluemound Road P.O. Box 13819 Milwaukee, WI 53213

ALL I ASK OF YOU

(From "THE PHANTOM OF THE OPERA")

Music by ANDREW LLOYD W

3
3

AVE MARIA

By FRANZ SCH

fz pp

con molto express.
simile

3 2 1 2
6
2
2
3 2 4
3
4 3
2

BECAUSE I LOVE YOU
(The Postman Song)

By WARREN ALLEN BR

To Coda
rit. (last time)
mp
1.
mf
2.
D.S. al Coda
CODA
(rit.)
Ped.

BRIDAL CHORUS
(From "Lohengrin")

By RICHARD W

mp

ENDLESS LOVE

By LIONEL RICHIE

cresc.
mp
cresc.
f

dim.
3
1
mp
dim.
2
mp
3
rit. e dim.
pp

DON'T KNOW MUCH

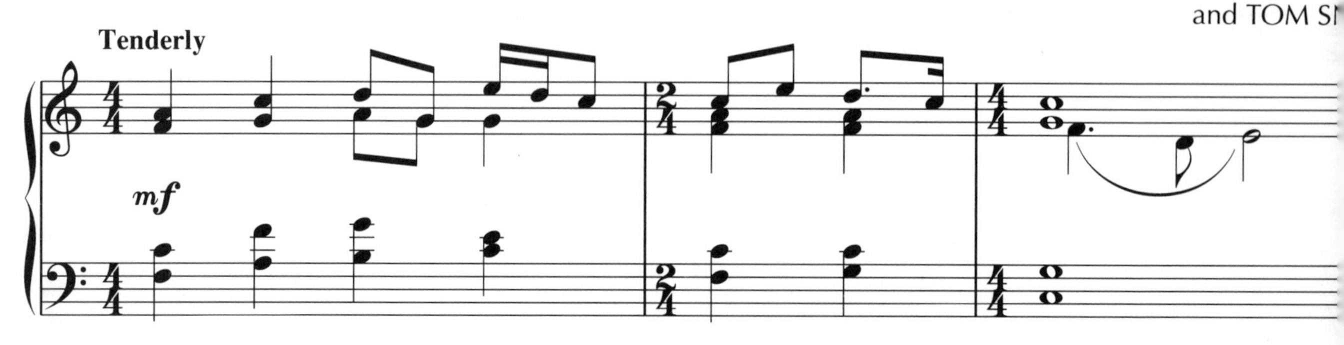

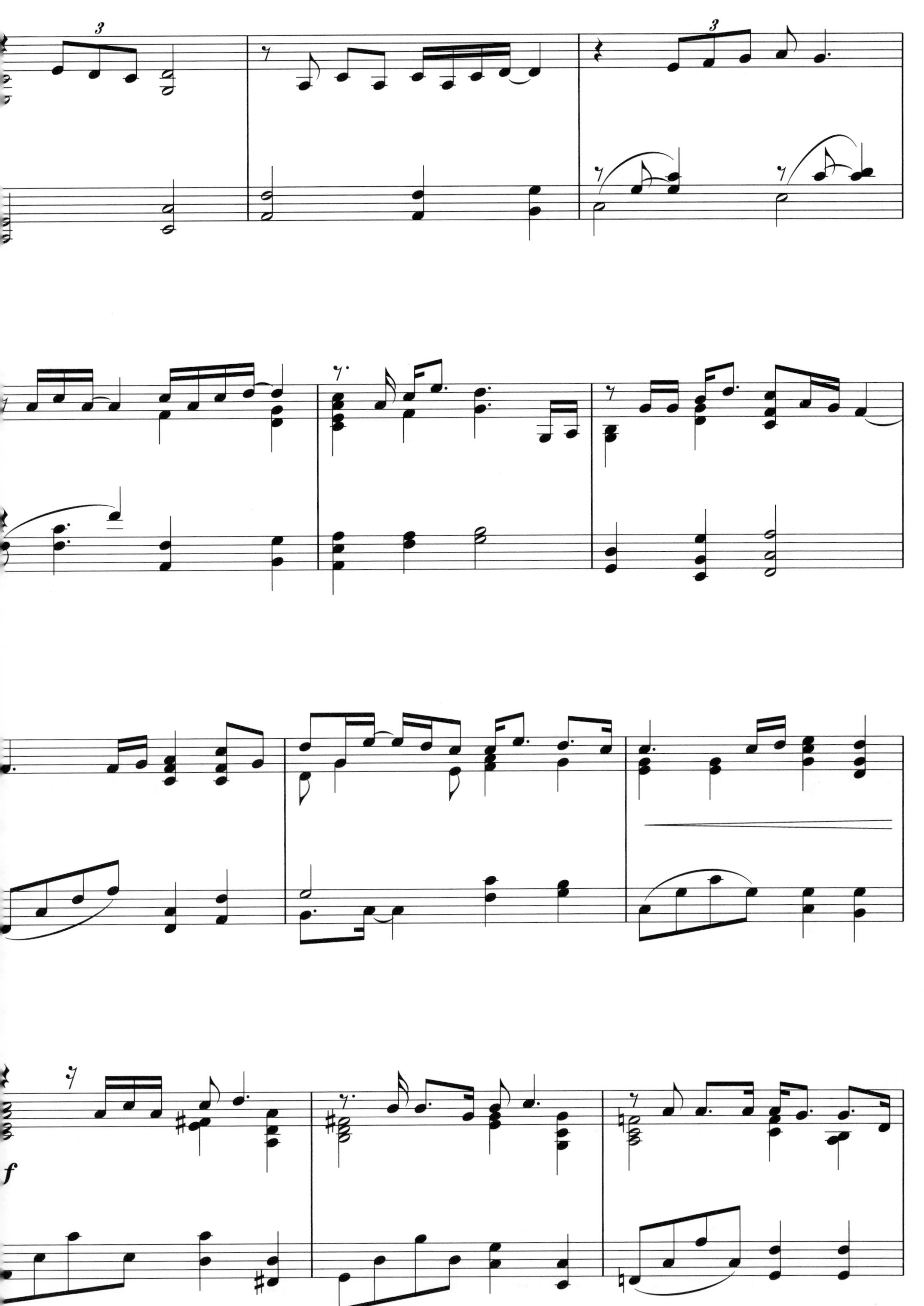
3
3
f

f
3
3
3
3
p
3
mp

mf
5
5
4
3
1
2
1
1
mp
2
4
rit.
Slowly
p
Ped.

FOR ALL WE KNOW

(From the Motion Picture "LOVERS AND OTHER STRANGERS")

Music by FRED

mp cresc.
mf

3
3

mp
f
rit. (2nd time only)
To Coda
D.S. al Coda
3
mp cresc.
CODA
Slowly
mp
p

HERE AND NOW

By TERRY STEELE and DAVID E

p
mp
mf
3

f

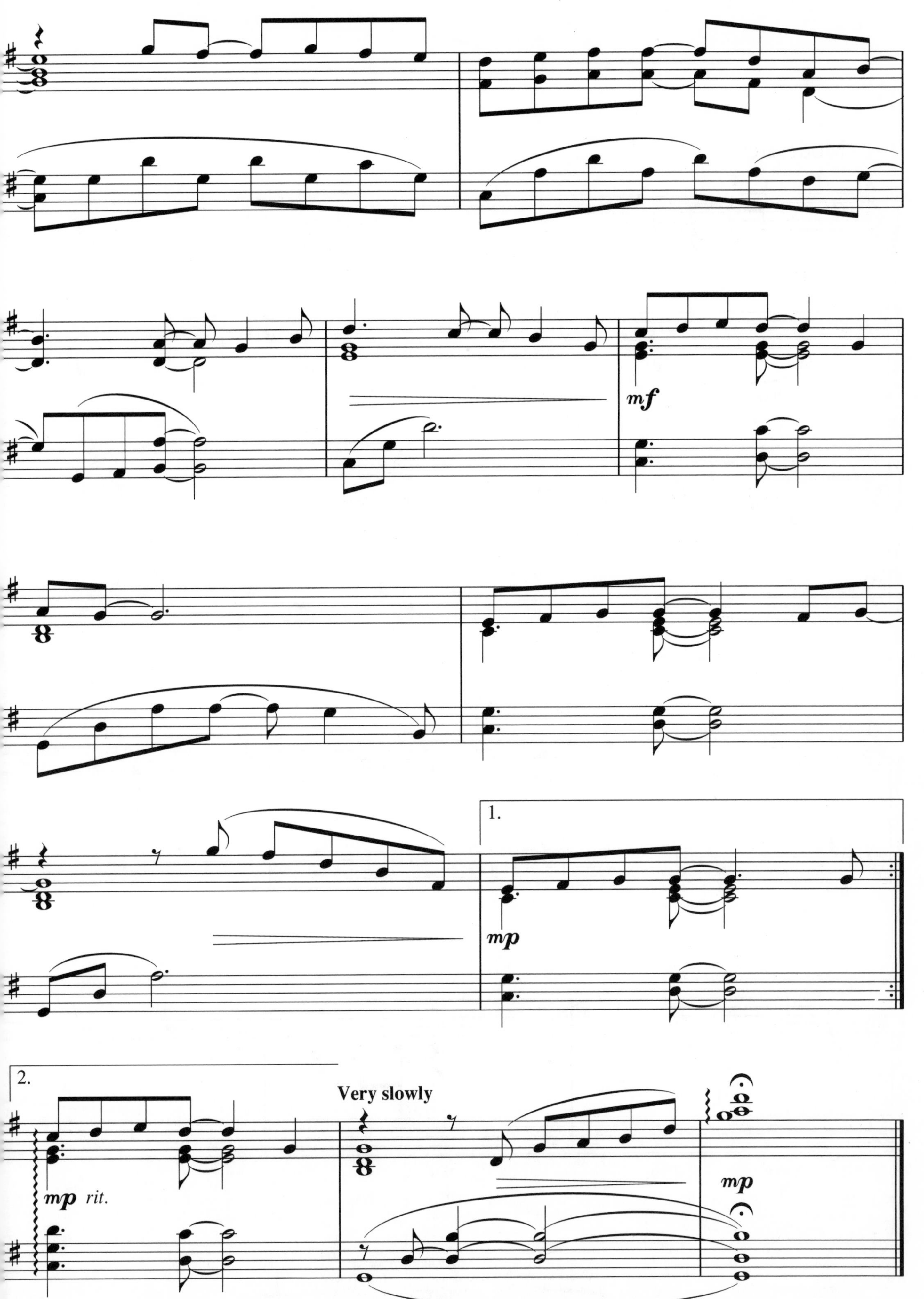
mf
1.
mp
2.
mp rit.
Very slowly
mp

JUST THE WAY YOU ARE

By BILLY

5
f

1
1

ff

mf
rall.

LONGER

Moderate ballad

By DAN FOGE

mf
p
mf
p
mf

8va
molto rit.
mf
a tempo
p
mf
p
loco

mf
p
mf
p
mf
slower
L.H.
rit.
p

LOST IN YOUR EYES

By DEBORAH GI

L.H.

6

I'LL BE LOVING YOU (FOREVER)

By MAURICE S

mf
To Coda
f

D.S. al
CODA
rit. (on repeat)
Freely
8va

THE MUSIC OF GOODBYE

(Love Theme From "Out Of Africa")

Music by JOHN BARRY

mf
p
rit.
pp

MORE
(Theme From MONDO CANE)

Music by RIZ ORTOLANI and NINO OLIV

mp
5 1 3 2 1 2 3 4
f
p cresc.

rit.
Rubato
(R.H.)
mp
8va
mf
p
R.H.
L.H.

SUNRISE, SUNSET
(From the Musical "FIDDLER ON THE ROOF")

Music by JERRY BOCK

8va

Moderate tempo

mf

f

rit.

a tempo

mf

2 1 3 1
4 1
f

Slower
rit.
mp
piu mosso
Animated
rit.
mf
simile
cresc.

f

rit.

Majestically

ff

mf

rit.

8va

dolce

mp

Cadenza

accel.

rit.

Presto

8va

ff

THE LORD'S PRAYER

By ALBERT HAY MAL

p
pp
molto rit.
mp
Ped.
L'istesso tempo
pp
expressively

p
poco accel.
rall.
pp
p
p
poco a poco cresc.
Ped.

Majestically, slightly brighter
f
2
3
5
1
3
5
1
2
3
5
f
Ped.
mf
p
rall. e morendo
pp
ppp
Ped.

SOMEWHERE IN TIME

By JOHN BA

3
3
mf
poco rit.
3
.H.
mp a tempo
3
cresc.
3
mf
mp
3

mf
3
3
f

3
3
poco rit.
8va
mp
Ped.

THROUGH THE YEARS

By STEVE DORFF and MARTY PA

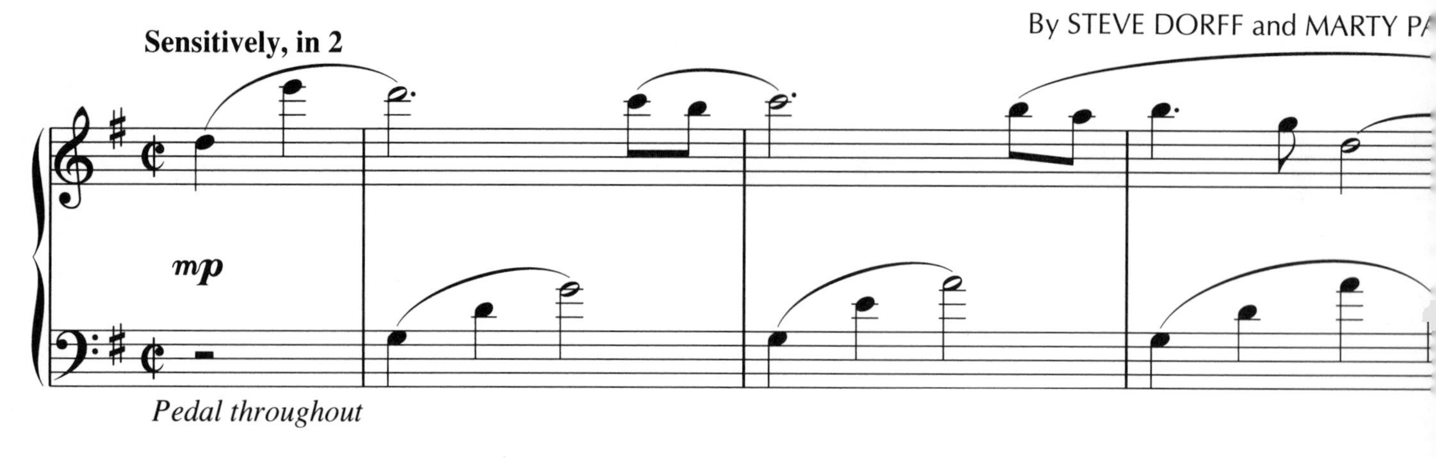

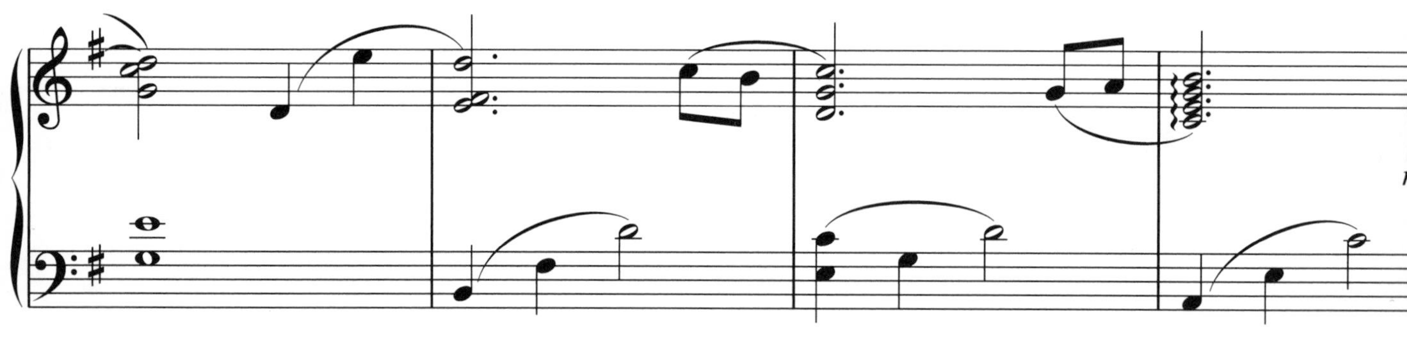

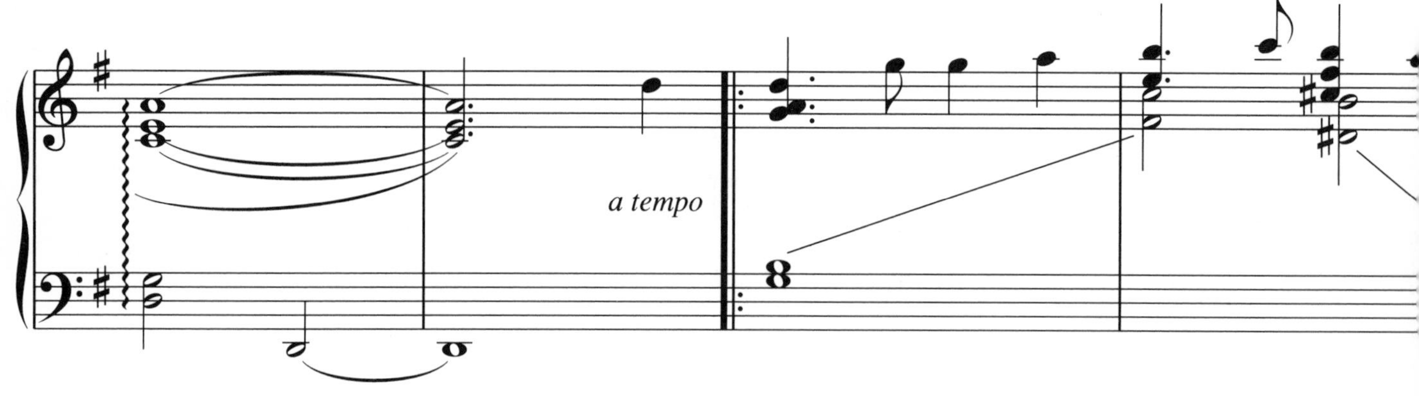

mf
rit.
a tempo
mp

mf

1.
mp
rit.
2.
a tempo
cresc.
f

mf
cresc.
f
8va
molto rit.
p
Ped.

UNCHAINED MELODY

Music by ALEX NORTH

mf
poco rall.
mf
a tempo
poco rall.

Piú animato
3
a tempo
poco rit.
mp
L.H.
3
3
Broadly
3
mf
3
3
f
poco allarg.
3

Cantabile
a tempo
mp
mf
cresc.

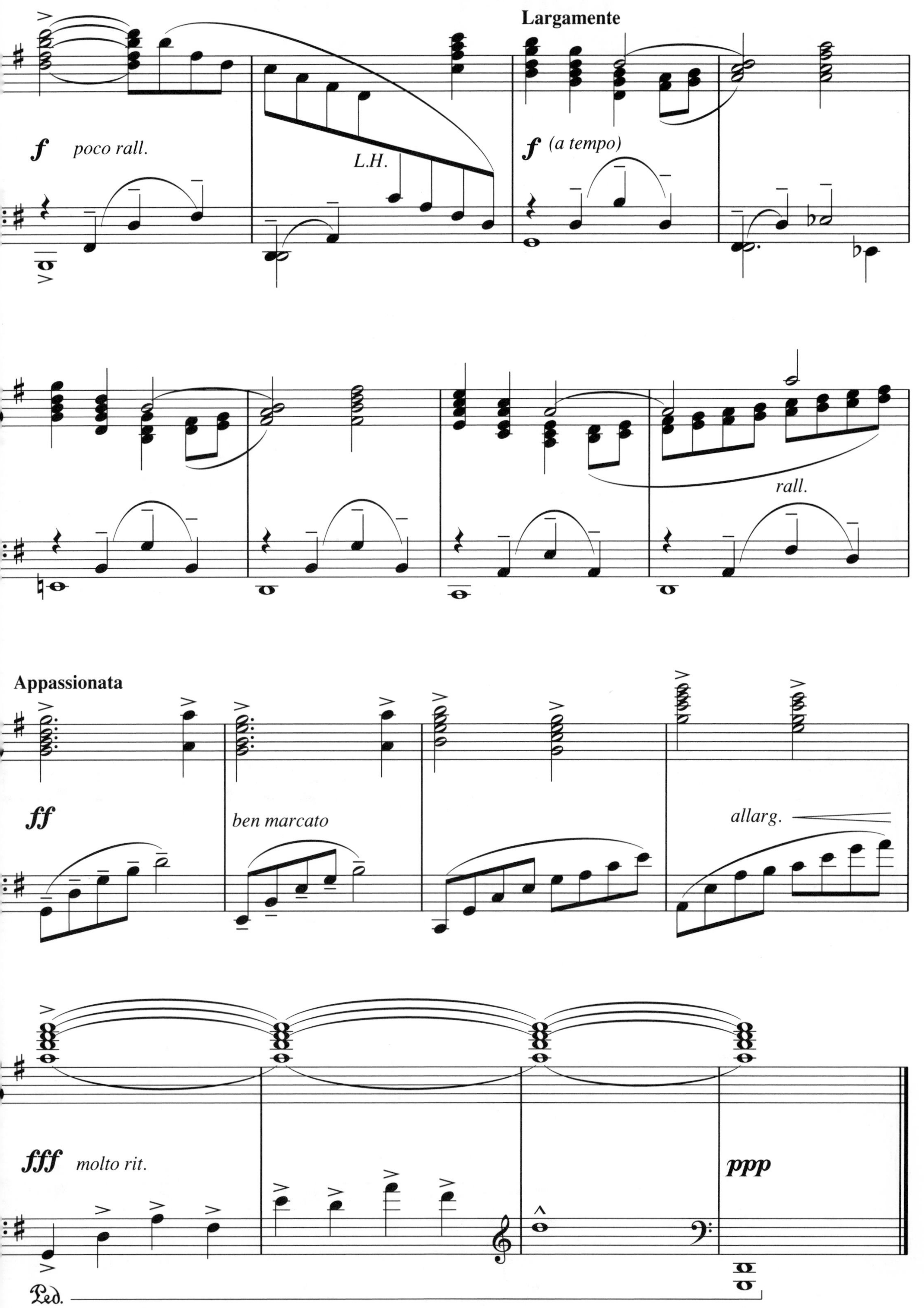
Largamente
f
poco rall.
L.H.
f
(a tempo)
rall.
Appassionata
ff
ben marcato
allarg.
fff
molto rit.
ppp
Ped.

VISION OF LOVE

By MARIAH C
and BEN MARG

Moderately slow, bluesy

mf

1.
2.

f
mf

rit.

THE VELOCITY OF LOVE

By SUZANNE C

Moderately

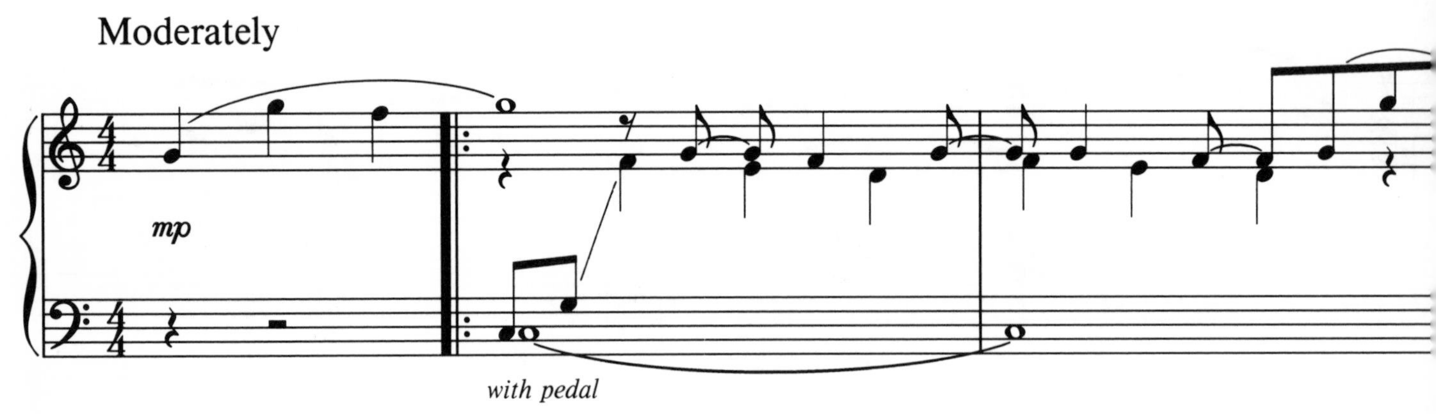

1.

2.
cresc.
f

8va
mf
p

f
mf cresc.
f
f

8va

8va

3

cresc.

mp

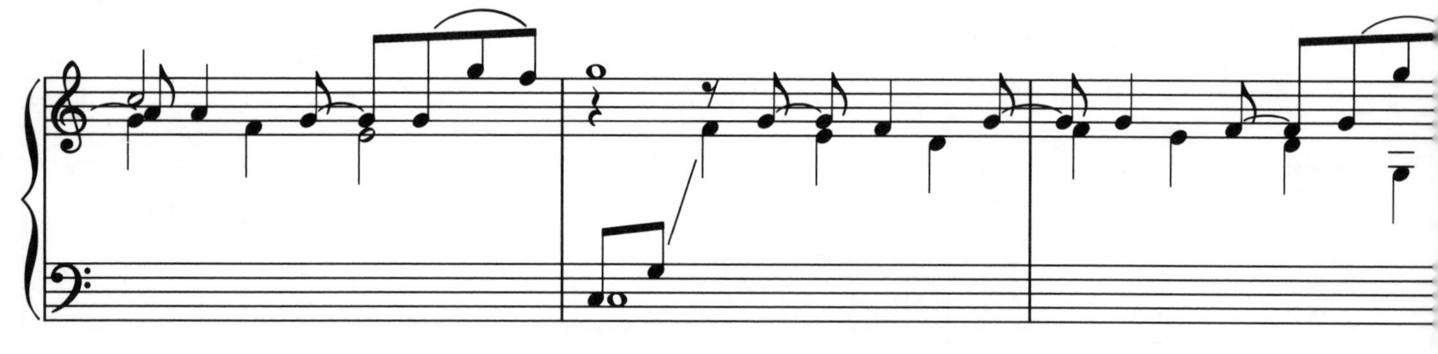

cresc.

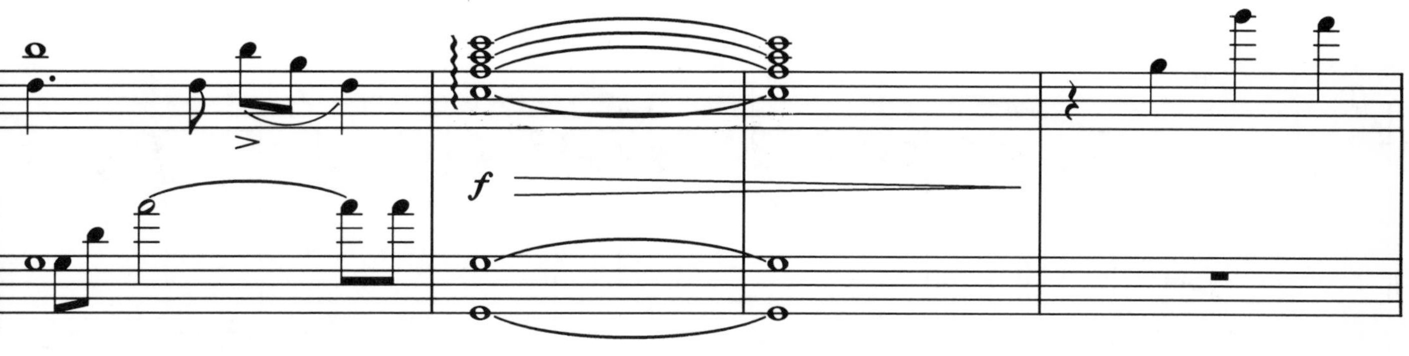
f

sfz
fading away
pppp
8va bassa

WEDDING MARCH

By FELIX MENDELSS

2.
1.
2.
To Next Strain
Fine
p

p
1.
2.
cresc.

molto cresc.
p
cresc.
D.S. al Fine

WHEN I'M WITH YOU

By ARNOLD DAVID L

1.
2.

3

WHITHER THOU GOEST

By GUY SIN

mf
mp

rit.
p
a tempo
mp poco a poco cresc.
mf

rit.
f
mf
mp
Very slowly
molto rit.
mf
mp
p

YOU NEEDED ME

By RANDY GOOD

4
5
f
2
1
mf
5
2
4-5
1
rall.
mf
a tempo
8va

8va
8va
8va
simile
8va
f
mf

rall.
f
Broadly
8va
f
8va
mf
ff
Freely, with excitement
Slower
dim.
rit.
mp
p
8va

THE VOWS GO UNBROKEN
(Always True To You)

By GARY BURR and ERI